Genre Expository Text

I0901329

Essential Question

How have people used natural resources?

The Spice Trade

by David Murphy

Introduction

These days, spices, such as pepper and cinnamon, are very common. They are available everywhere and are used in many of our meals. Hundreds of years ago, spices were very rare and were worth a lot of money. Explorers traveled long distances to search for them. Some people even faced danger and **risked** their lives to find spices.

Spices are a good example of how the desire for natural resources affects what people do. The value of those resources depends on three **significant**, or important, **principles**: supply (the amount available), demand (the amount people want), and price (how much people pay).

Spices can now be found in any supermarket.

Here is a modern example of supply and demand. A new cell phone comes out. But there are not enough phones for everyone who wants one. There is more demand than supply, so prices are high. At the same time, not many people want old cell phones. There is more supply than demand, so the price for the old phones is low.

Sometimes supply and demand are balanced, so the price settles in the middle. The history of the spice trade shows how supply and demand work.

SUPPLY AND DEMAND

The price of an item becomes steady when the supply and the demand for it meet.

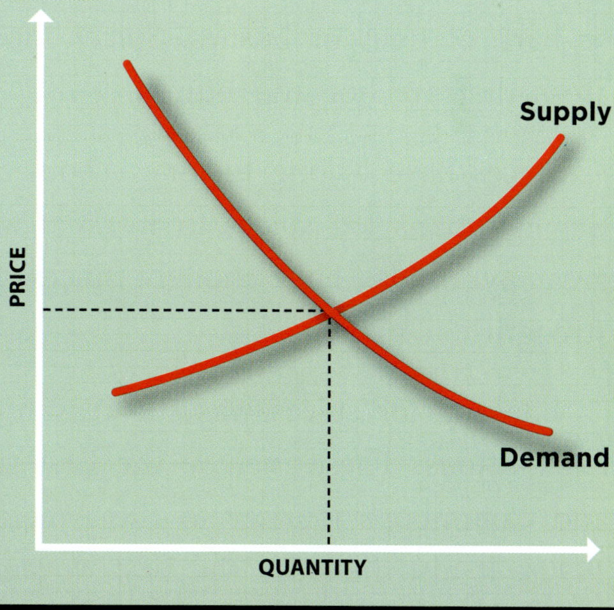

Black pepper starts as tiny berries on a vine.

CHAPTER ONE

A Reason for Discovery

Spices are a natural resource, which means they come from nature. They are usually the seeds, roots, or bark of trees or bushes. Spices mostly come from areas that are hot and humid.

Spices have a long history. About 5,000 years ago, the Egyptians fed spices to workers who built the great pyramids. They thought spices gave the workers strength.

Looking for spices was the reason for many famous explorations. These include the first trip around Africa and Columbus's journey to the Americas, both in the 1490s. It also includes the first **voyage** around the world in the early 1500s.

Long ago, most spices came from a group of islands in Indonesia. These islands were known as the Spice Islands. Spices also came from India.

Merchants from India and the Spice Islands brought pepper, cloves, nutmeg, mace, and ginger to the Middle East. They carried the spices in canoes across the Indian Ocean. Some spice traders also traveled over land by riding camels.

STOP AND CHECK

How did merchants bring spices to the Middle East?

ROUTES FROM THE SPICE ISLANDS TO EUROPE.

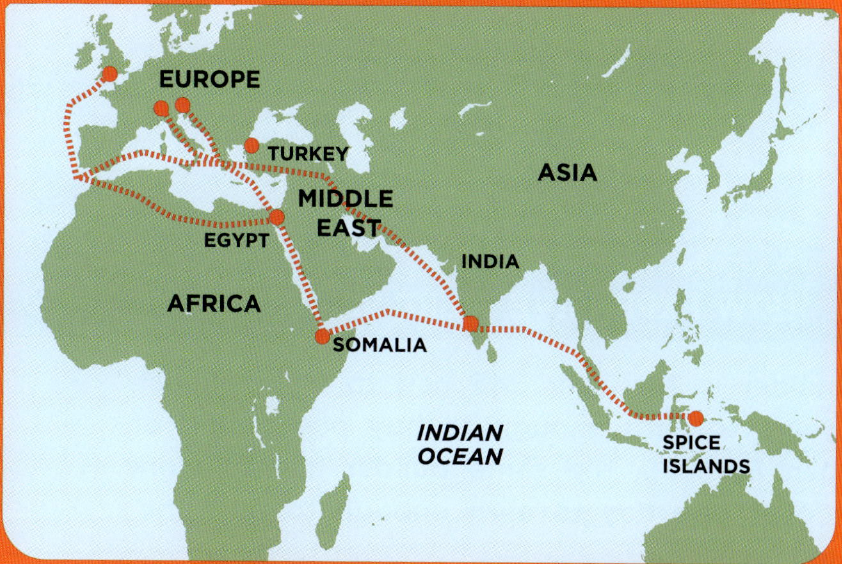

There were two main centers for the spice trade in the Middle East. One was Alexandria, Egypt. The other was Constantinople (now called Istanbul) in Turkey. Traders carried spices from these cities to North Africa, other cities in the Middle East, and Europe.

However, in the Middle Ages (around 500 to 1500 C.E.), trade between Europe and the Middle East was difficult. There were robbers, and transportation was slow. Trade became even more difficult in 1453. The Ottoman Turks took control of Constantinople. They closed off the overland route, or road, to Europe.

HOW EXPENSIVE WERE SPICES?

A builder in the year 245 had to work almost 19 years to earn enough to buy one pound of ginger. By 1875, the same builder had to work just over one day to earn enough to buy one pound of ginger.

DA GAMA'S ROUTE TO INDIA, 1498

Vasco da Gama

It took Vasco da Gama, the explorer, ten months to reach India in 1498.

Because the land route was closed, the only way to get spices to Europe was by sea. The rulers of Venice, in Italy, controlled the sea routes. They also controlled the **distribution** of spices, and they set high prices.

So, the Spanish and Portuguese looked for another trade route. In 1498, the Portuguese explorer Vasco da Gama sailed around Africa and reached India. Portuguese traders used this new route to bring spices from Asia, increasing the supply. The price of pepper in Portugal fell to one-fifth of the price in Venice.

STOP AND CHECK

How did the Portuguese lower the price of spices?

CHAPTER TWO
The Fight for Control

Now Portugal controlled the spice route to the east. Other countries had been looking for their own routes. An Italian explorer named Christopher Columbus thought he could reach India by sailing west. Spain agreed to pay for Columbus's voyage.

On October 12, 1492, Columbus reached the Bahamas in the Caribbean Sea. He thought that he had arrived in India. Columbus returned without any spices, but he had found lands the Europeans had not known about.

COLUMBUS'S VOYAGE, 1492

Christopher Columbus called the island where he landed San Salvador.

Columbus's journey made Spain want to find more new lands. At that time, Portugal was the **dominant**, or most powerful, ocean explorer. However, Spain was becoming stronger. In 1494, Portugal and Spain signed a **treaty** to stop fights over new **territories**, or areas of land.

This treaty created an imaginary line through the Atlantic Ocean. All lands discovered to the east of that line would belong to Portugal. Lands discovered to the west would belong to Spain.

In 1522, Spanish explorers **circumnavigated** the world. An explorer named Juan Sebastian del Cano returned to Spain with one ton of spices. The Spanish king gave him an **ornate** coat of arms.

The Treaty of Tordesillas divided new lands between Spain and Portugal.

Spain and Portugal continued to control the spice trade. This lasted for most of the sixteenth century. However, the Netherlands also wanted a share of the trade.

In 1602, the Netherlands created the Dutch East India Company (DEIC). This company had thousands of ships and a huge number of workers. It became the world's largest spice trader for over a hundred years.

Then around 1770, a Frenchman stole some clove plants. He planted them in some French island colonies near the eastern coast of Africa.

The Dutch East India Company had 50,000 workers.

As a result, other people could get clove plants and grow them. This destroyed the Dutch **monopoly**. Soon spices were being grown all over the world.

New ships were built to sail the new trade routes. These ships were fast and safe, and they had large **holds** for the spices. Captains **replenished** their supplies and returned home much more quickly. There were more spices to sell, so spice prices fell sharply.

Spices were once a **luxury**, or treat. Only very wealthy people could afford them. Today, spices are a **commodity** that can be found in any supermarket.

STOP AND CHECK

How did the Netherlands take control of the spice trade?

CHAPTER THREE
The Demand for Spices

Why was there such a high demand for spices? It was because they were used for many important purposes. Throughout history, spices have been used in religion, medicine, business, and cooking.

Spices in Religion

The Egyptians used cassia when they made mummies. Thousands of years ago in **ancient** Greece, people believed that spiced wine had religious qualities.

Today, turmeric is still used in Hindu rituals. In Judaism, spices are used as part of the *havdalah* ceremony at the end of the Sabbath.

Archaeologists found 3,000-year-old spices in a pharaoh's tomb.

Spices in Medicine

An Egyptian **papyrus** written around 1500 B.C.E. names the spices coriander and cumin. They were used for medicine.

The ancient Greeks ate ginger wrapped in bread to improve digestion.

Ancient Greek doctors used spices for medical purposes, too. They used ginger to improve digestion. Nutmeg was used to make the spleen stronger, and pepper was used to treat coughs and colds.

Spices are still used in many **remedies**, or treatments, today. In Asian medicine, pepper is used to treat problems with digestion, breathing, and the heart. It has even been used to treat hair loss!

Spices as Money

In the Middle Ages, people used dried peppercorns as money. They used the spice to buy goods and to pay taxes and rents.

Peppercorns were still being used as money in 1545. This is the year that the British warship the *Mary Rose* sank. In the 1980s, scientists found peppercorns in the wrecked ship when it was taken out of the water.

Epics/Hulton Archive/Getty Images

The *Mary Rose* was buried in mud. This helped preserve its cargo of peppercorns.

Calicut, India, has been an important part of the spice trade for more than 500 years.

Spices in Cooking

In cooking, spices have always been used to make food tastier and more **edible**. For example, pepper has been used to flavor food in India for thousands of years. It is even mentioned in a poem called *The Mahabharata*. This poem was written in India in the fourth century B.C.E.

STOP AND CHECK

How do we know that peppercorns were used as money in the 1500s?

SAFFRON—LIGHT AND EXPENSIVE

Saffron comes from a flower called the saffron crocus. It is the most expensive spice in the world.

Farmers make saffron by drying the **stigmas** of the flowers. It takes 50,000 to 75,000 plants to make a pound of saffron. One pound of dried saffron can sell for as much as 5,000 dollars!

Growing Saffron

1. Farmers plant the saffron crocus bulbs at the beginning of fall.
2. The next fall, the crocus bulbs produce flowers.
3. Farmers collect the flowers by hand.
4. Each flower's stigmas are taken out by hand and dried over charcoal embers.

Conclusion

Spices are a regular part of our lives today. In the past, however, this natural resource was in very high demand and cost a lot. Spices **symbolized** wealth. They showed others that you were rich and important.

The spice trade has a long history. People traveled around the world to find spices. They risked their lives and discovered new lands.

Even today, spices can remind us of travel and adventure. The smell of vanilla, nutmeg, or cinnamon can make us think of distant islands and brave explorers racing across the sea to these faraway lands.

Today spices are used in dishes all over the world.

Respond to Reading

Summarize

Summarize how spices became everyday items. Use details from *The Spice Trade*. Your graphic organizer may help you.

Main Idea
Detail
Detail
Detail

Text Evidence

1. Reread pages 6 and 7. One reason spices were expensive in Europe was that getting them was difficult. What key details support this idea? **MAIN IDEA AND KEY DETAILS**

2. Find the word *distant* on page 17. What clues help you to figure out the word's meaning? **VOCABULARY**

3. Reread Chapter 3. Write about one way spices have been used throughout history. Include details from the text. **WRITE ABOUT READING**

Genre Myth

Compare Texts

Read about how Heracles used a river to clean some stables.

The Greek myth of Heracles tells the story of impossible tasks he completed. *A Clean Sweep* is a satire of three of these tasks. Satire is the use of humor to point out a person's flaws.

A Clean Sweep

Heracles had a terrible temper. King Eurystheus told him he had to learn to control himself if he wanted to be a god.

"Sometimes I think your brain is **impenetrable**," the king said with a sigh. "If you want to be a god, you must complete one of three tasks without losing your temper. The first task is to slay the Hydra. Every time you cut off its head, two more heads will grow."

By that afternoon, Heracles had cut off 50 of the Hydra's heads. Now it had 100 more, and Heracles was furious.

Then, an owl flew onto Heracles's shoulder. The owl was wearing glasses. He whispered to Heracles that he knew the answer.

"Don't tell me what to do!" Heracles yelled.

The next day, King Eurytheus said to Heracles, "You should have listened to Noctua the owl. Only one of the Hydra's heads was alive. Noctua would have told you which one. Your next task is to kill a savage lion."

Heracles did his best, but the lion had solid gold fur. Every time Heracles hit the lion, he broke his sword.

Noctua appeared and whispered, "Thrust your sword into the lion's mouth."

"Don't tell me what to do!" Heracles shouted.

Illustration: David Sheldon

"You should have listened to Noctua," King Eurytheus said the next day. "Your last task is to clean the stables of King Augeas. If you lose your temper again, you'll never be a god."

Soon Heracles stood in front of the stables. Noctua flew onto his shoulder.

"Fine," Heracles said. "Tell me the answer."

But Noctua dropped his glasses into the mud. "I can't see anything now," the owl said.

"I can see enough!" Heracles said. "There's a river running beside the stables. If I change its direction, it will flow through the stables and wash all the dirt away."

The water flowed through the stables and washed the dirt away. But Heracles was washed away with it, yelling all the way.

"Ah, Heracles," King Eurystheus sighed. "When will you learn?"

Make Connections

What natural resource did Heracles use to clean the stables? **ESSENTIAL QUESTION**

Why are natural resources important in *The Spice Trade* and *A Clean Sweep*? **TEXT TO TEXT**

Glossary

circumnavigated *(sur-kuhm-NA-vuh-gayt-uhd)* traveled all the way around ***(page 9)***

holds *(hohldz)* cargo storage areas ***(page 11)***

merchants *(MUHR-chunts)* people who buy and sell goods for profit ***(page 5)***

monopoly *(muh-NAHP-uh-lee)* complete control over the market for a good or service ***(page 11)***

papyrus *(puh-PIGH-ruhs)* a thick paper-like material made from the papyrus plant ***(page 13)***

principles *(PRIN-suh-puhlz)* basic laws or truths ***(page 2)***

stigmas *(STIG-muhz)* upper parts of the female part of the flower ***(page 16)***

treaty *(TREE-tee)* a formal agreement between two or more countries ***(page 9)***

Index

Focus on Social Studies

Purpose To research one of the spices in this book.

What to Do

Step 1 Work in pairs. Choose a spice from *The Spice Trade.*

Step 2 Find out more about the spice. When was the spice discovered? What plant does it come from? Where did it first grow? What was the climate like in that place? Show this place on a world map with color and a label.

Step 3 Is the spice grown in more places today? Add these places to your world map. Use a different color and label for each place.

Step 4 Share your map with the class.